Simply Science

POWERFUL MACHINES

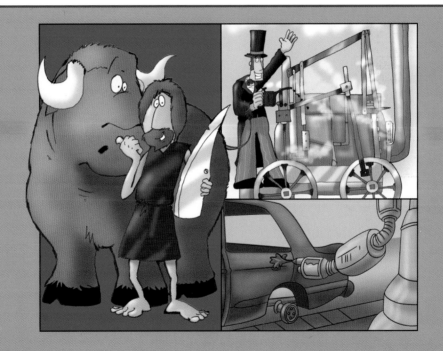

Gerry Bailey

Illustrations: Steve Boulter & Q2A media

Diagrams: Karen Radford

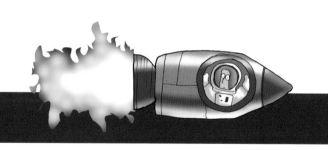

AUTHOR: GERRY BAILEY

CONSULTANT: STEVE WAY

EDITOR: FELICIA LAW

ILLUSTRATORS:

STEVE BOULTER

Q2A MEDIA

DESIGN: RALPH PITCHFORD

ISBN 978-1-906292-19-5
Printed in China

PHOTO CREDITS:

p.5 Sharon Meredith/Shutterstock Inc.
p.8 Alan Egginton/Shutterstock Inc.
p.10 Jeff Gynane/Shutterstock Inc.
p.15 Carolyn M. Carpenter/Shutterstock Inc.
p.17 Ponomareva Yevgeniya/Shutterstock Inc.
p.19 (bl) John Leung/Shutterstock Inc.,
(tr) S.H.K./CORBIS SYGMA.
p.20 (l) Uli/Shutterstock Inc.
p.20-21 qaphotos.com/Alamy.
p.22 (t) Gary L. Brewer/Shutterstock Inc.
(b) Thomas Sztanek/Shutterstock Inc.
p.23 (tl) Craig Aurness/CORBIS.
(cl) Chris Alan Wilton/Alamy,
(r) ESA/CNES/ARIANESPACE-Service Optique CSG.
p.26 Y. Shira/Rice University.
p.27 (t) Scott Bauer/US Department of
Agriculture/Science Photo Library,
(br) Eye of Science/Science Photo Library.
p.29 (tl) Evening Standard/Getty Images,
(tr) Oliver Uhrig/Shutterstock Inc.

Cover
p.5 Sharon Meredith/Shutterstock Inc.

POWERFUL MACHINES

Contents

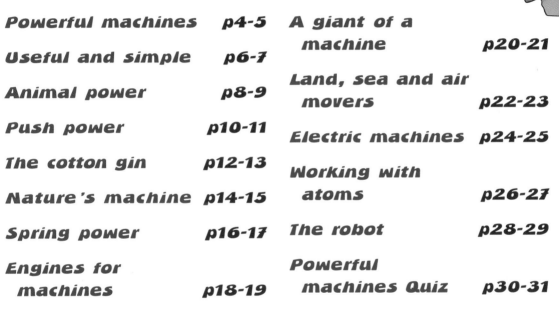

Powerful machines

What do you think of when you think of a really useful machine? You probably think of a machine that helps your mum or dad do things around the house, like a washing machine or a power drill. But you might think of something far simpler, like a corkscrew or a hammer. These are machines too.

Larger machines often need electricity or some other kind of energy to power them. But simple machines just need someone like you to move them.

Machines can be powered by **You** ...

    ... by an **ox** or a **horse**

        ... or by the **Sun**.

They can be powered by **electricity** ...

    ... by burning a fuel like **petrol**

        ... by making **steam**

           ... or perhaps by **nuclear power**.

Useful and simple

Machines don't have to be big to be useful. Almost all machines are based on some very simple ones: we call these the 6 simple machines. You can find them in almost every tool and machine you use.

the lever

the wheel and axle

the pulley

the wedge

the ramp

the screw

Six simple machines

The six simple machines are:
the lever
the wheel and axle
the pulley
the wedge
the ramp
and the screw.

A pick axe

A pick axe works as a lever and a wedge. You power the pick axe into the ground like a big hammer. But the end piece is shaped into a wedge that drives apart the earth or stones as it hammers down.

Tin opener

A tin opener is three simple machines in one. The handle you squeeze works as a lever. It pushes a little wheel with a sharp rim into the tin. The rim is a wedge. Then a wheel and axle turns the machine so that it cuts around the top of the tin and opens it.

handle

sharp rim of wheel

A screwdriver

A screwdriver uses twisting power to ease a screw into a material. It's really just a long screw by itself. The screw's thread, or ridge, acts like a long ramp to ease the screw into the material slowly, one full turn at a time.

A claw hammer

A claw hammer works as a lever to bang nails into wood or some other material. You use your arm as part of the lever when you hammer. The 'claw' part pulls out nails. It's the load end of the lever this time. The top of the hammer-head is the fulcrum.

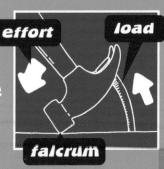

effort

load

falcrum

Animal power

A plough is a tool that carves a groove, or furrow, in a field to make it ready for seeds to be sown there.

A plough has a handle for guiding and a blade that acts as a wedge. This pushes the earth apart and then turns it over.

Oxen or horses pulled the first ploughs. These early ploughs were probably made in China and parts of the Middle East. Farmers still use ploughs today, but most modern ones have many rows of steel blades and are pulled by powerful tractors.

1. When people began farming, they probably just threw the seed onto the ground and waited. But sometimes the crows ate the seed. It needed to be sown deeper in the ground.

A wedge for ploughing the land

2. A pointed stick could make deep holes for the seeds to be dropped into. But it would take a long time to plant seeds this way.

3. The farmer could use the stick to scrape a furrow. This would work but the furrows might not be deep enough.

4. An axe would be strong enough to hack holes or furrows in the hard ground. The wedge shape of the blade would cut through the earth easily.

5. If this wedge was then attached to a wooden frame, it could be yoked to a strong animal and pulled along by it.

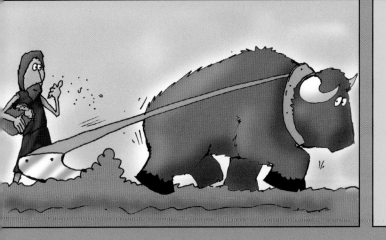

Push power

A wheelbarrow is a machine that is made up of two simple ones – a lever and a wheel and axle.

The axle is actually the fulcrum of the lever while the wheel works to cut down rubbing, or friction.

Simple machines work together to make a task easier for us to do.

A lever helps raise loads – the handle of the wheelbarrow is the lever.

A wheel and axle helps move loads smoothly along the ground.

1. Long ago if people wanted to move something from place to place, they had to carry it or balance it on their head.

2. Later, people used a kind of wheel-less wagon. It was just a box on runners that could be dragged along. You could carry more in this, but it was still hard work.

A wheel that helps carry loads

3. When the wheel was invented, things began to change. Large wagons could be pulled by horses. But could a much smaller kind of wagon be invented where the load was spread round the wheel and a person could push it along?

4. The answer was to build a board around a wheel and axle, and add handles. This was the simple tool that became the first wheelbarrow.

5. In the modern wheelbarrow, a V-shaped frame is fixed to the wheel and axle. The box, or 'barrow', now fits onto this frame and handles are attached to the end.

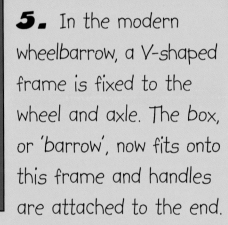

The cotton gin

Cotton is a plant that is harvested each year and used to make a special fabric.

It's cotton-pickin' time again!

The pickers used to remove the seeds from the fluffy cotton seeds, or bolls, as they picked. This was a lot of trouble and took a long time.

A tool that cleans cotton

1. By the late 1700s, cotton was a popular fabric for clothing in America and demand was high. Eli Whitney lived in the south where a lot of cotton was grown.

2. But there was a problem. It took the pickers a whole day to separate out the seeds as they gathered in the cotton.

12

How the gin worked

The cotton gin was a very simple invention. The cotton bolls were put into the top of the machine. As the handle turned, the cotton fed through wire teeth that combed out the seeds. Then a brush roller removed the cotton from the wire teeth.

cotton bolls
wire tooth roller
brush roller
seeds

3. It would be far quicker to remove the seeds by machine – some kind of mechanical brush. Unfortunately, nothing like this had been invented.

4. But Eli Whitney came up with the idea of a brush-and-roller machine. He made a cylinder with wire teeth to pull the fibres through tiny holes. Then he added a roller with brushes to remove the fibre from the teeth. The rollers were wound with a handle. His cotton gin was a huge success.

Nature's machine

The sundial is one of the earliest tools. It is used to tell the time of day. It is usually made from a short pillar with a marked, round top.

A pointer shaped like a slanted triangle is fixed to the middle of the plate. It's called a 'gnomon'.

A shadow that tells the time

1. In olden times, people used the Sun to guess what time of day it was.

2. But the Sun couldn't be used to record exact hours and minutes.

3. However, people noticed that it did cast shadows as it moved position during the course of the day. Maybe this shadow could be used to record the passing hours...

Casting a shadow

Around the top of the sundial is a time scale marked in hours. When the sun shines it makes the pointer, or gnomon, cast a shadow onto the time scale showing what hour it is. As the sun moves, the shadow moves around the dial.

...special times like when you had to feed the animals or do the housework...

... or the time it took to make a long journey.

4. This led to the invention of the sundial. A round plate, was marked like a clock face with the hours. A pointer in the middle cast a shadow. It was easy to read which hour the shadow fell on.

A portable time tool

1. Ever since clocks were invented, people had been able to tell the time accurately in minutes and hours.

2. As long as you could see a clock, you knew what time it was. If not, you still risked being too late or early.

3. Clocks used weights called pendulums to power them. These were sometimes as large as a person.

4. So unfortunately, if you wanted to be sure of the time, you had to carry your heavy clock around with you all day - not very easy at all!

5. Of course, you could make a special harness for this, but it would obviously be better to have a smaller clock powered by something lighter than a pendulum.

Spring power

A wristwatch is a tool for telling time that is worn on the wrist. It uses a small coiled spring for its power.

How does a spring work?

A spring is a coiled piece of flat wire. If you push the spring out of shape, it always goes back to how it was. In other words, it 'springs' back. A spring that is pushed out of shape has energy which is stored up ready to use. This energy is turned into movement when the spring is released. The first watches used this kind of energy for power.

6. The coiled spring was the answer. It could be very small and has energy stored in it. The spring was used to power tiny clocks that could be worn on a chain or on the wrist. They were called watches.

Many clocks and other gadgets use coiled springs to move the parts inside.

Engines for machines

Machines are wonderful things, but large machines need more than muscle power from humans and animals – even a spring coil – to make them work. They need a much stronger source of power to keep them moving. They need an engine!

The petrol engine

A petrol engine is actually called an internal combustion engine, or an engine that makes an explosion inside. A mixture of air and petrol cause the explosion. The explosion pushes down pistons that turn a crank. The crank is connected by a shaft to the wheels of the car.

The steam engine

The first steam engines were very large and not very efficient. But Richard Trevithick's high-pressure steam engine changed all that. It was small enough and powerful enough to be used in mines, and to help develop the steam locomotive and the railway system.

The electric engine

When Michael Faraday invented his dynamo, or electricity making machine, he also made it possible to invent an electric motor. Electricity and magnetism are used to make a rod turn, which can operate a piece of machinery, such as a sewing machine or a fast train.

Fast electric trains can move at speeds of more than 560 kilometres per hour!

The atomic engine

Scientists discovered that when the nucleus, or middle part, of an atom is split, it makes a huge amount of energy - in other words, a very big blast. This blast of energy can be used to power engines - if you're very careful! Atomic, or nuclear, submarines use atomic-powered engines to turn their propellers.

A *giant of a machine*

Sometimes, if you want to do a big job, you have to have a big piece of machinery to do it. A really huge machine like this rock drill, is designed to cope with some pretty tough work.

This huge machine is an earth mover, or excavator. It moves heavy soil and rock from one place to another.

Machines make up many forms of transport. These are getting faster and faster as new kinds of energy and technical gadgetry are discovered to power them forwards.

Goods trains can pull hundreds of coaches. The train carrying iron from Zouerate to the coast in Morocco, is probably the world's longest train. It can stretch to as long as 3 kilometres!

The Terex Titan is the World's largest **dump truck**. It can carry huge loads up to 350 tonnes. It has wheels that are 3.3 metres high.

Supertankers weigh thousands of tonnes. These are the world's largest ships, able to transport two or three million barrels of oil across the seas.

The world's biggest plane is the Russian built **Antonov 225** which carries air cargo. It can carry 80 cars!

The **Ariane rocket** needs a huge amount of power to thrust it into space.

Electric machines

Most of the machines we see around the house and in schools or offices, are powered by electricity.

Electricity is generated by spinning a wire coil between two big magnets – called a generator. The coil is spun around by a turbine which can be driven by wind, water or steam. The electricity generated, called mains electricity, is distributed to your home by a network of metal cables.

Electricity can also come from a battery. A battery turns chemical energy into electrical energy.

Mobile phones

A mobile or cell phone is actually a small radio, or walkie-talkie. It is an electrical machine that sends messages along sound frequencies that are picked up and passed on from one transmitter to another. The transmitters are located in a particular area known as a cell. The cells are then linked so that messages can pass from cell to cell as you move and talk.

A pacemaker

If you have a heart problem, a pacemaker might help your heart to function properly. It's powered by a small battery and sends electrical impulses to the heart to help it beat more regularly.

A computer

Computers use a "binary" code of on and off electrical pulses. The first computers used large vacuum tubes to make the on/off digital pulses, so the computers were huge – the size of rooms! In 1947, small on-off switches called transistors were invented that allowed computers to be made smaller and faster. Then "microchips" with several tiny transistors clustered together on each microchip appeared. To begin with there were about ten transistors on each microchip – now there can be a billion!

ATV

An Advanced Tethered Vehicle, or ATV for short, is an unmanned electric-powered submersible used for exploring wrecks lying on the seabed.

Imagine a machine so small you can't actually see it. In fact it's so small you'd get 20,000 of them side by side on a human hair. This incredible machine is a nanomachine. And it's created through a process called nano-technology.

Nano (or tiny) -technology means working with things measured in nanometres. A nanometre is one billionth of a metre - and that's very, very small!

Everything we see around us, from huge trees to tiny moths, were built one atom at a time. So scientists believe they should be able to invent things by building them one atom at a time as well. And that's nano-technology. An atom, in case you were wondering, is ten nanometres wide.

Nano-car

The funny looking machine below is actually a tiny car - a nano-car. It was built from just a few atoms. It has a rotating motor that's powered by light. It has a chassis and four axles and spherical molecule wheels.

And it's just 4 nanometres long!

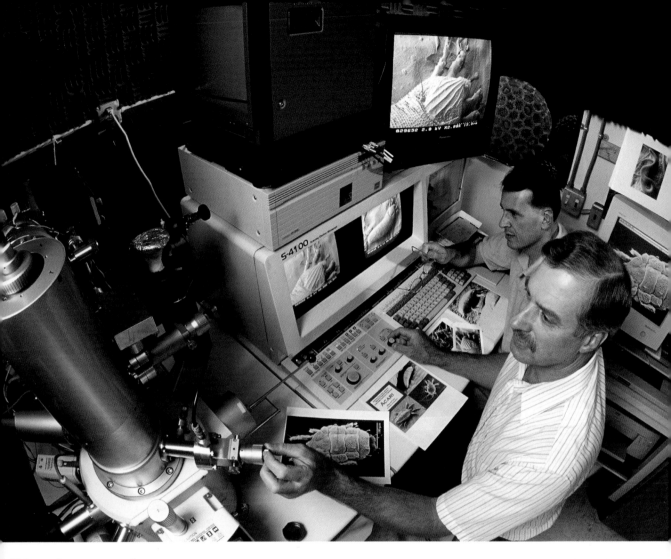

Electron microscopes

Electron microscopes use beams of tiny parts of an atom called electrons. The electron beams magnify objects far more than normal microscopes, so we can see what's inside our cells, even what chemicals like DNA look like!

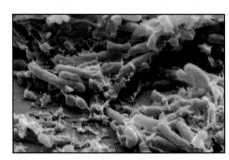

Tiny bacteria can be seen using an electron microscope.

The robot

A robot is a machine that can do jobs without any help from humans. Some carry out repetitive tasks, while others do dangerous jobs, such as working inside nuclear reactors or with harmful liquids.

The word 'robot' comes from the Czech word 'robota', which means hard work.

A machine to do routine jobs

1. In large factories, hundreds of workers are needed to do lots of different jobs. Some of these are very boring and take up a great deal of the worker's time.

2. The bosses try to make these jobs more interesting. But they also want to find a way of cutting costs. Hiring workers to do such easy, routine jobs is expensive.

The first robot

At first, scientists competed to develop robots that would help them in other fields. In 1932, a robot called Alpha was shown in London that could read, bow, tell the time, sing and smoke cigars!

Alpha

Large mechanical robots are assembled side by side to perform simple tasks in a car factory.

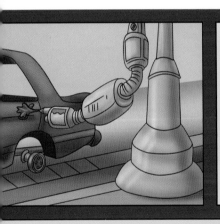

3. Inventors came up with a machine that could do repetitive jobs such as painting, or welding panels on cars.

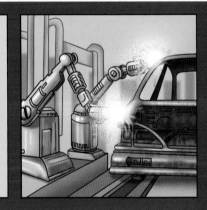

4. These machines are known as robots. They follow a series of instructions that are programed into them. Usually a robot contains a computer called the control system. This acts like an electronic brain. The computer program makes the robot repeat and check the automatic tasks.

Powerful Machines Quiz

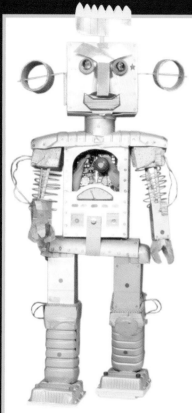

1. How many simple machines help make a tin opener?

2. What kind of machine is used to dig tunnels?

3. How long is a nanometer?

4. What type of machine gets the seeds out of cotton fibres?

5. Which electric machine helps keep the heart beating?

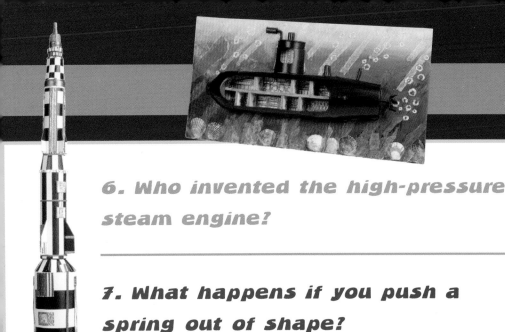

6. Who invented the high-pressure steam engine?

_____

7. What happens if you push a spring out of shape?

_____

8. What two machines make up a wheelbarrow?

_____

9. Will a sun dial gnomon work in the dark?

_____

10. When does an ox pull a wedge?

_____

1. There are six 2. A rock drill 3. It's one billionth of a metre 4. A cotton gin 5. A pacemaker 6. Richard Trevithick 7. It returns to it's original shape 8. A wheel and axle and a lever 9. No it won't it needs sunlight 10. When it's hitched to a plough

Index